MW00830069

In God's Image

In God's Image

Janet Neff Brewer

Bridge Resources
Louisville, Kentucky

Special thanks to the friends and family of Bridge Resources whose faces you see on these pages.

Edited by Virginia Watkins

Book interior and cover design by Pamela Ullman

Illustrations by Pip Pullen

Photography by Geoffrey Carr

First edition

Published by Bridge Resources
Louisville, Kentucky

PRINTED IN THE UNITED STATES OF AMERICA

98 99 00 01 02 03 04 05 06 07 — 10 9 8 7 6 5 4 3 2 1

Web site address: http://www.bridgeresources.org

Library of Congress Cataloging-in-Publication Data

Brewer, Janet Neff, date.
　　In God's image / Janet Neff Brewer. — 1st ed.
　　　　p.　　cm.
　　Summary: Presents a Christian view of sexuality as well as simple explanations of how babies are conceived and born and how to take care of one's body.
　　ISBN 1-57895-055-4
　　1. Sex—Religious aspects—Christianity—Juvenile literature. 2. Sex instruction for children.
[1. Sex—Religious aspects—Christianity. 2. Sex instruction for children. 3. Christian life.]　I. Title.
BT708.B75　1998
241'.66—dc21
　　　　　　　　　　　　　　　　　　　　　　　　　　　　　　　　　　98-13165
　　　　　　　　　　　　　　　　　　　　　　　　　　　　　　　　　　AC

A Note to Parents

You are your child's first and most important teacher. How exciting! And sometimes, how frightening. Because you know your young child better than anyone else, you have both the responsibility and the opportunity to teach your child about his or her sexuality. As you do this, you are not only teaching biological facts, but you are also teaching your child values. This book was written to help you teach those facts and values from a faith perspective.

Your child will not necessarily understand or be interested in all the information presented here at one time. That's just fine. You may want to concentrate on reading the parts of the book that are most interesting to your child at the time and simply talk about the pictures in the rest of the book. Children's understandings keep expanding as they mature. This is a book you can return to often throughout your child's early years. It is also a book that you and your young child can share together, as well as one that your child can enjoy looking at alone.

You will find more help in teaching your child about sexuality in *In God's Image: Young Children and Sexuality—Parent's Guide*, which is available through Curriculum Publishing, Presbyterian Church (U.S.A.); (800) 524-2612.

In the guide you will find activities you can do with your young child, as well as help in dealing with many of the situations and questions relating to young children and sexuality.

One of the most important things parents can do for their children is to come to them with a spirit of openness, acceptance, and willingness to meet their needs. By establishing yourself as an approachable parent and taking advantage of those teachable moments when your child is very young, you are encouraging your child to also come to you for information and guidance as he or she grows older.

Y ou are very special because God made you. When you were a little baby, you couldn't do much except sleep and eat and laugh and cry. You needed people to take care of you.

Y ou needed someone to give you food, change your diapers, and keep you warm and dry. Someone had to carry you everywhere you went.

As you get older, you learn to do some things for yourself. You learn to crawl and walk, to use the bathroom, and to feed yourself. Sometimes you choose which clothes you will wear.

No matter how big you get or how much you can do for yourself, you will always need people to love you. That's what families are for.

Dear God, thank you for making me. I know you're helping me to grow. Thank you for people who love me and take care of me. Amen.

F amilies come in all shapes and sizes. What kind of family did God give you?

Any kind of family can be a good family if they love and take care of one another. God put us in families so we will have people to love and people who will love us.

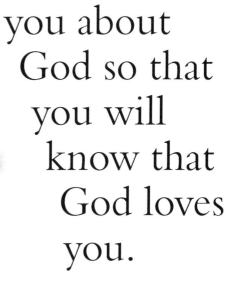

God also wants us to be part of a church family. The church family loves you, takes care of you, and teaches you about God so that you will know that God loves you.

Thank you, God, for my family. Help me to show the people in my family that I love them. Thank you for people in my church family who love me. Amen.

G od made us all and gave us good bodies. Some people are tall and some are short. Some people are thin and some are round. Some have curly hair and some have straight hair. God gave each of us the body that is just right for us.

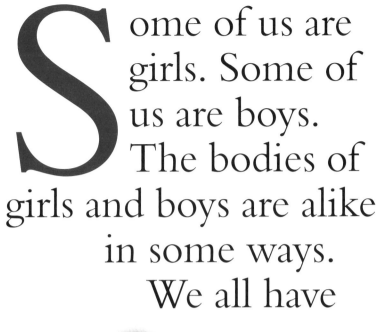

S ome of us are girls. Some of us are boys. The bodies of girls and boys are alike in some ways. We all have eyes, arms, and toes. How else are the bodies of girls and boys alike?

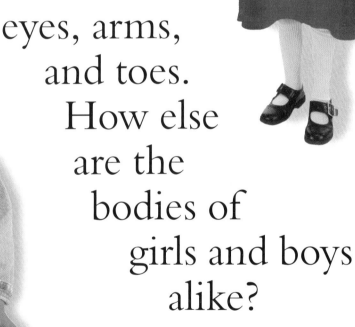

The bodies of girls and boys are different in other ways. A girl has a *vulva*, a *vagina*, and a *uterus*. Her vagina and uterus are inside her body where we can't see them. These body parts are private and are just for her.

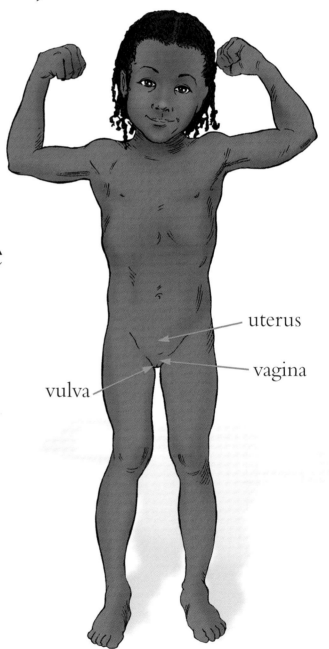

uterus

vagina

vulva

A boy has a *penis* and a *scrotum* with two *testicles* inside it. These body parts are private and are just for him.

Thank you, God, for all kinds of body parts. You put us together in just the right way. Thank you for making me the way you want me to be. Amen.

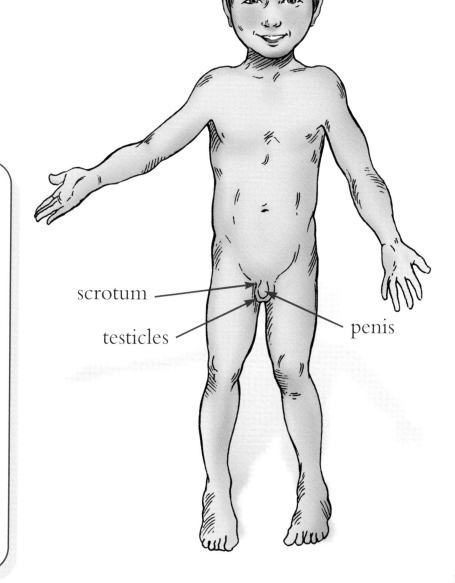

scrotum

testicles

penis

Sometimes when boys grow up into men and girls grow up into women, they find a person to love in a special way and decide to get married. A husband and wife may want to have a baby to share their love.

A baby lives inside the mother's body in a special place called the uterus for about nine months. The mother's body gives the baby everything it needs while it grows.

Finally, the happy day comes when the baby is born. A baby is a wonderful gift from God! Now both the mother and father can take care of the baby.

Our bodies are gifts from God, and God wants us to take care of them. Some of the ways to take care of your body are to brush your teeth, eat foods that make you healthy and strong, and get plenty of exercise and sleep.

Doctors and nurses also help us to take care of our bodies. We go to the doctor for checkups, shots, or when we are sick or hurt.

Taking care of your body also means doing things to be safe. It's important to know people who will take care of you and help you to be safe. Ask your mom and dad to tell you who those people are.

Thank you, God, for all the people who take care of me and help me to be safe and healthy. Help me to learn to take care of my body and keep it safe. Amen.

Touching is an important thing. There are many kinds of touches. Some touches, like hugging and snuggling, make us feel good. What kind of touching do you like to do in your family?

If someone touches you in a way that makes you feel scared or mad, tell the person to stop. Then get away from that person and tell your mom or dad or another grown-up. Your body is special. It belongs to you, and God doesn't want anyone to do anything to hurt your body.

Has anyone ever told you something and told you not to tell anyone else? That's called keeping a secret. Some secrets are good, and it's fun to keep them. But sometimes it's not good to keep secrets. If you're not sure whether you should keep a secret or not, ask one of your parents or another grown-up to help you decide.

God gives us all kinds of feelings. Part of growing up is learning the best ways to show your feelings. When you're feeling happy, you want to tell someone. It's good to share things with people who can be happy with you.

When you're feeling sad, you should also tell someone how you feel. The people who love you want to know when you are sad so they can help to make you feel better.

W hen you're mad, you might want to hit someone or throw something. These are not the best ways to show that you're angry. Try telling another person why you feel mad. Maybe you can work something out so you won't be mad anymore.

Everyone is afraid of something sometimes. Are there things that make you feel afraid? When you're afraid, sometimes it helps to tell another person how you feel.

One of the best gifts that God gives us is the feeling of love. We need other people to love us, and we need to love other people. Feelings are an important part of people. It's good that God gives us so many different feelings.

Thank you, God, for giving us feelings. I know you care about me when I'm sad and like to see me happy. Help me to find healthy ways to show my feelings. Amen.

God made each of us special and a little different from everyone else. There are many different people in the world, and no one else is exactly like you. You are very special! And God loves you.

Thank you, God, that you made me special and there's no one else exactly like me. Help me to be just what you want me to be. Amen.